GRADES
1–2

Brighter Child®
An imprint of Carson-Dellosa Publishing LLC
Greensboro, North Carolina

Brighter Child®
An imprint of Carson-Dellosa Publishing LLC
P.O. Box 35665
Greensboro, NC 27425 USA

Printed in the USA • All rights reserved.   ISBN 978-1-62057-660-1
01-002131151

Table of Contents

Introduction

Every day, your child encounters language arts in many different situations. The activities in *Creative Kids Language Arts* make learning these skills fun no matter what he or she is doing!

In this book, your child will:

- Read stories about Max and Emma and practice language arts skills by drawing illustrations and answering questions about key details in the text.

- Play fun language arts games that help your child identify parts of speech, vowels and consonants, types of sentences, and punctuation.

- Learn about liquids and solids, space, parts of a flower, and volcanoes— which helps to strengthen his or her reading comprehension, classifying, and writing skills.

- Create sock puppets, stages, and treasure maps while reading step-by-step directions and writing imaginative narratives.

Max's Map

"Hi Emma," Max called. "Look what I found in my backyard!"

"That looks like a pirate's map!" Emma said.

"Let's follow it and see where it goes," Max said.

"Maybe we will find treasure!" Emma said.

Directions: Color Max and Emma.

"There are a lot of steps to follow," Max said.

"Let's start at the tree," Emma said. She pointed to the big tree in Max's backyard.

"Good idea," Max said. He carefully held the map. "First, we need to take 10 steps toward the swings."

Directions: Help Max and Emma read the map. Draw the path they should take. Follow the directions below.

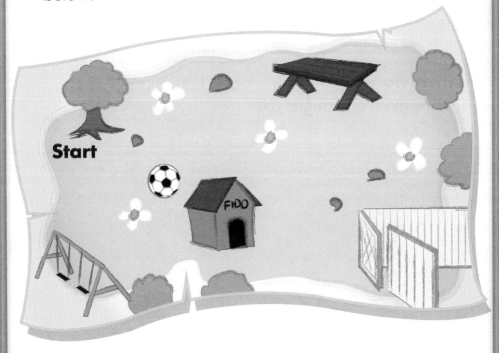

Start at the tree. Walk to the swing set.

Next, walk past the doghouse.

Then, turn and walk around the **red** table.

Walk straight down to the gate.

"Looks like we need to go through the gate," Max said.

"The treasure must be in my backyard!" Emma exclaimed. They walked into Emma's yard.

"Uh oh," Max said. "We have to cross a river!" He pointed toward the little pool for Emma's baby brother.

"Just like real pirates!" Emma said.

Directions: Imagine Max and Emma are pirates. Draw them crossing a river.

"Look!" called Emma. "X marks the spot!" She pointed to a big X drawn in the sandbox.

"Let's start digging," Max said excitedly.

"I found a treasure box," Max said. "And it has my name on it!"

"I wonder what is inside?" Emma asked with a smile.

Directions: What do you think Max's treasure is? Draw it in the treasure box.

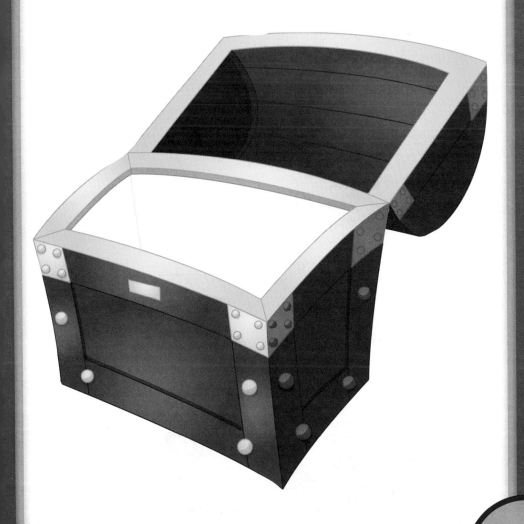

"Did you like your pirate's map, Max?" asked Emma.

"Yeah! That was fun," Max said.

"Good, maybe I will make you another one," Emma said.

"You made the map?" Max laughed. "I want to make one for you first!"

Directions: Review the story. Write your answers on the lines.

Whose backyard does the map start in?   **Max's**

Emma's

What do Max and Emma pretend
to be when they cross the pool? _____

Who made the treasure map? _____

Language Arts Games

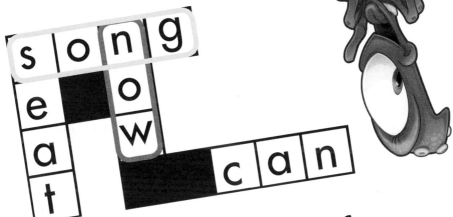

S N A I L

Earth

Crack the Code

Directions: Use Max and Emma's secret code to unlock a silly but true statement. A **statement** is a telling sentence that ends with a period (**.**).
Add a period to the end of the statement after you break the code.

A	B	C	D	E	F	G	H	I	J	K	L	M

N	O	P	Q	R	S	T	U	V	W	X	Y	Z

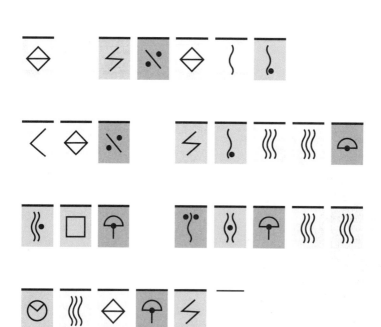

A SNAIL CAN SLEEP FOR THREE YEARS

Space Nouns

Directions: Find the out-of-this-world space nouns from the word box. Remember, **nouns** name a person, place, or thing. Words can be across, down, or diagonal.

```
c  s  t  b  n  o  j  r  p  i
z  h  c  s  k  i  e  s  k  d
x  i  g  p  w  s  u  h  n  v
t  p  l  a  n  e  t  q  e  s
o  u  y  c  l  m  n  a  a  t
r  a  a  e  c  i  h  e  r  o
e  w  e  c  s  r  e  j  t  s
i  e  u  r  s  l  k  n  h  u
s  v  r  l  w  d  g  f  a  l
c  x  g  m  a  r  s  n  r  a
```

space	earth	planet
skies	stars	mars
alien	ship	

Hidden Picture

Directions: There are six nouns hidden in Max's backyard. Find and circle them. What other nouns do you see?

butterfly	apple	beach ball
baseball bat	frog	turtle

Crack the Code

Directions: Use Max and Emma's secret code to unlock the answer to a question. A **question** is an asking sentence that ends with a question mark (**?**). Fill in the missing question mark below. Then, solve the code to find the answer!

How do you take a sick pig to the hospital _____

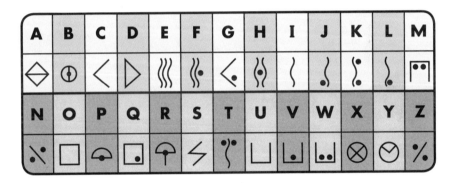

Spelling: Word Scramble

Directions: Look at the pictures and words. The words are all scrambled up! Spell the words correctly on the lines.

rutkc

_____

ynra

_____

frgiafe

_____

likm

_____

Vowel Maze

Directions: Help Max answer a riddle. Follow the vowels **a**, **e**, **i**, **o**, and **u** through the maze to find the answer.

What kind of key will not open a door?

Crack the Code

Directions: Use Max and Emma's secret code to unlock the answer to a question. Fill in the missing punctuation for the question and answer.

Why did the banana go to the doctor ____

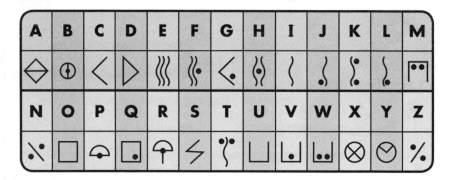

 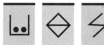 

Proper Nouns

Directions: A **proper noun** names a special person, place, or thing. It starts with a capital letter. Read each riddle below. Find and unscramble the correct proper noun from the word box. Be sure to start with the capital letter!

rMas	rEath
nuS	nruSat

This huge star lights the day.

___ ___ ___

This is our home planet. ___ ___ ___ ___ ___

This planet is red. ___ ___ ___ ___

This planet has rings. ___ ___ ___ ___ ___ ___

Adjective Word Search

An **adjective** is a word that describes a noun. It tells more about a noun, like **yellow** duck or **hard** rock. Adjectives can answer the question **what kind?**

Directions: Find the adjectives from the word box. Words can be across or down. Then, think of a noun each adjective could describe.

q	r	e	d	z	b	b
o	d	s	a	d	j	h
l	n	w	h	l	t	o
d	i	s	s	q	e	t
c	c	g	r	e	e	n
r	e	y	u	m	a	f
s	m	o	o	t	h	n
x	k	s	p	i	c	y

red	smooth	green
hot	spicy	sad
old	nice	

On the Playground

When writing sentences, it is important to use **subject-verb agreement**. When a sentence is about one person or thing, add **s** to the verb, such as the leaf blow**s** away. When a sentence is about more than one person or thing, do not add **s** to the verb, such as the cats look for mice.

Directions: Fill in the verbs below with your own silly ideas. Then, write them in the story. Be sure to use correct subject-verb agreement.

Verb (action word) _____

Verb (action word) _____

Verb (action word) _____

Finally, the recess bell rings! First, Emma

_____ to the swings. Max
      verb

and his friends start a game of tag. Max

_____ right into Emma! Then,
      verb

Max and Emma _____ a ball
                 verb

back and forth before it's time to go back inside.

Spelling: Word Scramble

Directions: Look at the pictures and words. The words are all scrambled up! Spell the words correctly on the lines.

 gsrsa

_____

 **rebda**

_____

 **pzirep**

_____

 hrtea

_____

Crossword Puzzle

Directions: A **noun** is a person, place, or thing. A **verb** is an action word, like **jump** or **swim**. Finish writing the nouns and verbs from the word box in the puzzle. Circle the nouns in **blue** and the verbs in **green**.

ran	last	legs	digs
gate	camp	rest	sip
sat	pen	end	kick

Riddles

Directions: An **adjective** describes a noun. It tells more about a noun, like **big** dog. Read the riddles below. Circle the adjectives. Then, draw a line from the riddle to the answer.

My big body is heavy.
I lived a long, long time ago.
What am I?

My tall neck is long.
I eat leaves from trees.
What am I?

I have long ears.
I hop very fast.
What am I?

Space Nouns

Directions: Find the out-of-this-world space nouns from the word box. Words can be across or down.

```
o  i  t  w  s  m  c  v  j  k
g  a  l  a  x  y  l  o  l  p
s  b  c  g  p  c  t  m  a  n
n  k  s  p  g  e  r  c  s  s
w  v  l  b  r  o  c  k  e  t
u  f  o  u  i  q  w  r  r  a
e  k  z  t  m  e  t  e  o  r
t  a  x  x  a  n  c  u  j  g
q  j  f  g  f  p  b  n  l  r
l  i  g  h  t  e  t  t  w  s
```

galaxy	rocket
laser	light
star	meteor

Max and Emma Go to the Fair

Directions: Fill in the nouns, adjectives, and verbs below with your own silly ideas. Then, write them in the story. Be sure to use correct subject-verb agreement.

Noun (a thing) _____

Verb (action word) _____

Adjective (describing word) _____

Max and Emma are at the fair. First, they go

see the _____. Max is so
noun

excited he _____ the whole way
verb

there! Emma stops to buy a _____
adjective

cotton candy. They love coming to the fair!

Matching Game

Directions: Cut out the cards below and on page 29. Mix up the cards and place them facedown. Turn two cards over, one at a time. Try to match two rhyming words together. If no match is made, flip both cards back down. Continue flipping and matching until all the cards are paired.

hat	snake	fan
box	spoon	mop
flag	clock	log

Matching Game

Directions: Cut out the cards below and on page 27. Mix up the cards and place them facedown. Turn two cards over, one at a time. Try to match two rhyming words together. If no match is made, flip both cards back down. Continue flipping and matching until all the cards are paired.

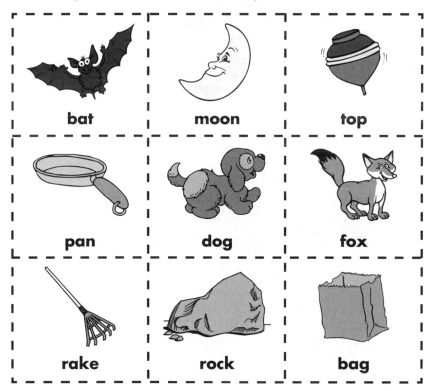

bat	**moon**	**top**
pan	**dog**	**fox**
rake	**rock**	**bag**

Crossword Puzzle

Directions: Finish writing the words from the word box in the puzzle below. Circle nouns in **orange** and verbs in **purple**.

bike	lake	feet	seed
ride	mule	bone	
gate	dive	rule	

Animal Riddles

Directions: Draw a line from the riddle to the correct answer. Circle the verb in each sentence.

I love to slide on the ice.
What am I?

I slither on the ground because I have no arms or legs.
What am I?

I hop on lily pads in a pond with my webbed feet.
What am I?

Crack the Code

Directions: Use Max and Emma's secret code to unlock the answer to a joke. An **exclamation** is a sentence that shows excitement or surprise. The answers to many jokes end with exclamation points (**!**). Add an exclamation point to the end of the sentence after you break the code.

Why was the baby ant confused?

A	B	C	D	E	F	G	H	I	J	K	L	M
◇	⊕	<	▷	≈	⦙	<.	◊	(	⸴	⸲	⸲	⊡

N	O	P	Q	R	S	T	U	V	W	X	Y	Z
✗	□	⌓	⊡	⊤	⚡	⸾	⊔	⊔·	⊔··	⊗	⊘	%

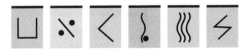

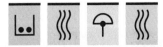 

Maze

Directions: Help Emma answer a riddle. Draw a line through the maze to find the answer. What other adjectives could describe the answer?

What is orange and sounds like **parrot**?

Start

End

Reveal Hidden Picture

Directions: Color all of the vowels **a**, **e**, **i**, **o**, and **u black** to discover something hidden in the puzzle.

j e j g w d q n j c g c u b
k g u m b j h c h w l o d s
r c z i l p q s b k i n z f
g k w x e d a e f e l x q k
v r f j p i o u a g n f s b
d n v m a e e i u u h b s f
u a e i e u a i u e a e i u
l z k i u u a a e e i m w z
q h r a e u e i a e e c c b
i u u e o a o u o i i o o u
t x b h a i e o u a d v r l
c h f s j e i e i f f k j v
n m d t e g a o t i j m x h
t p g i c v h n g d o p r l
l h o k q f r p s j t u g v

Crossword

Directions: Finish writing the words from the word box in the puzzle below. Use **blue** to circle nouns, yellow to circle verbs, and **red** to circle adjectives.

cat	pops	song	zoo
fog	fan	pear	tan
car	pig	hop	blue

Matching Contractions

A contraction is a way to join two words together. It is a shorter way to say something. An apostrophe (') takes the place of the missing letters. For example, **isn't** is a contraction of the words **is not**.

Directions: Draw a line to match each pair of words to its contraction.

Spelling: Word Scramble

Directions: Look at the pictures and words. The words are all scrambled up! Spell the words correctly on the lines.

 **pgersa**

_____

 **mneoyk**

_____

 **olgio**

_____

 **grof**

_____

Max's Invention

Directions: Fill in the nouns, adjectives, and verbs below with your own silly ideas. Then, write them in the story. Be sure to use correct subject-verb agreement!

Noun (a thing) _____

Adjective (describing word) _____

Verb (action word) _____

Adjective (describing word) _____

Max made an invention to help feed his dog.

He used _____, duct tape,
                          noun
and rope to make it. Emma came over to see his

_____ invention. Max and
           adjective
Emma _____ it outside.
               verb
His _____ dog sniffs it.
       adjective
Now, Max just needs to test it out!

Crossword Puzzle: Synonyms

Directions: Synonyms are words that mean the same or almost the same thing, like **dad** and **father**. Write the synonyms in the puzzle below. Use the word box to help you.

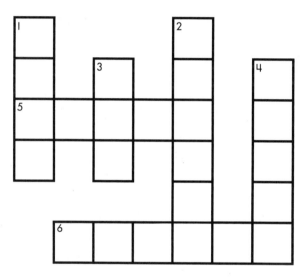

Across

5. synonym of **yell**

6. synonym of **tired**

Down

1. synonym of **quick**

2. synonym of **small**

3. synonym of **leap**

4. synonym of **glad**

fast	hop	little
shout	sleepy	happy

Maze

Emma has a riddle for you! See if you can find the answer.

Directions: Solve Emma's riddle. Draw a line through the maze to find the answer.

Start

What has bark, but no bite?

Verb Word Search

A **verb** is an action word. It tells what happens in a sentence, like Max **kicks** the ball or Emma **laughs** at the joke.

Directions: Find the verbs from the word box. Words can be across or down. Then, try to use each verb in a sentence.

r	p	s	t	s	c	d
e	f	o	b	w	l	j
a	e	t	s	i	n	u
d	c	l	i	m	b	m
p	s	x	n	k	h	p
r	g	o	g	r	w	s
u	f	d	d	r	a	w
n	r	c	w	a	l	k

walk	swim	climb
sing	draw	run
read	jump	

Riddles

Directions: Read the riddles below. Circle the adjectives. Then, draw a line from the riddle to the answer.

I have eight long arms.
I can blend in with the ocean floor.
What am I?

I am a very slow swimmer.
My short tail pushes me through
the water upright.
What am I?

I have very sharp teeth.
If you see my fin in the water,
swim away.
What am I?

Crossword Puzzle

Directions: Synonyms are words that mean the same thing, like **glad** and **happy**. **Antonyms** are words that are opposites, like **yes** and **no**. Write the antonyms in the puzzle below. Use the word box to help you.

Across

1. antonym of **low**
2. antonym of **no**
4. antonym of **empty**
6. antonym of **loose**

Down

1. antonym of **light**
3. antonym of **dangerous**
5. antonym of **right**

| high | safe | left | full |
| heavy | yes | tight | |

Hidden Picture

Directions: There are eight nouns hidden in the jellybeans. Find and circle them.

orange	pencil	strawberry
cherry	sharpener	tennis ball
cookie	**pink** bow	**blue** marble

Tongue Twisters

Directions: Read the tongue twisters below out loud. Can you say them fast three times? Then, write your own tongue twister on the lines!

She sells seashells by the sea shore

Black background, **brown** background

Black back bat

Six slimy snails sailed silently

_____

_____

Word Search

Directions: Use a **red** crayon to circle the names of three animals that would make good pets. Use a **blue** crayon to circle the names of three wild animals. Use an **orange** crayon to circle two animals that live on a farm. Words can be across or down.

bear	lion	bird	cow
cat	sheep	dog	tiger

```
a   m   e   o   w   w   n   l   i   o   n
b   m   d   o   g   g   x   i   i   s   o
a   b   e   a   r   r   v   l   m   h   r
r   m   r   m   o   o   u   s   e   e   k
k   c   a   b   b   i   r   d   s   e   m
i   o   t   t   i   g   e   r   m   p   q
b   w   n   o   w   w   r   q   n   e   n
d   n   c   p   h   h   i   d   u   d   n
f   k   c   a   t   t   r   o   a   r   m
```

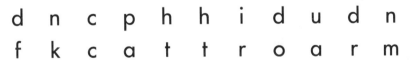

Emma's New Pet

Directions: Fill in the nouns, adjectives, and verbs below with your own silly ideas. Then, write them in the story. Be sure to use correct subject-verb agreement!

Noun (animal) _____

Adjective (describing word) _____

Verb (action word) _____

Noun (thing) _____

Emma has a new pet. It is a _____!
                                       noun

Max is playing with it, too. He gives the pet a

_____ toy. Emma _____
    adjective   **verb**

with her new pet. She gives it a new

_____. Now, it just needs a name.
   noun

48

Vowel Maze

Directions: Follow the vowels **a, e, i, o,** and **u** through the maze to help the monkey find the bananas.

Spelling: Word Scramble

Directions: Look at the pictures and words. The words are all scrambled up! Spell the words correctly on the lines.

 enska

_____

 clcok

_____

 apepl

_____

 eter

_____

Create Your Own Sentence

Max and Emma want you to write a secret sentence! Give your coded-sentence to a friend.

Directions: Use Max and Emma's code key to create your own secret sentence in the space below. Be sure to end it with a period, question mark, or exclamation point.

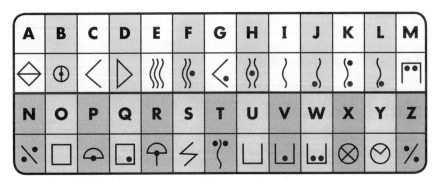

Snow Day!

Directions: Fill in the nouns, adjectives, and verbs below with your own silly ideas. Then, write them in the story. Be sure to use correct subject-verb agreement!

Adjective (describing word) _____

Verb (action word) _____

Noun (person or thing) _____

Verb (action word) _____

Max looks out the window, it snowed last night and school is cancelled! He runs outside to play

in the _____ snow. Emma
adjective

_____ outside. They start
verb

building a _____ out of
noun

snow. They _____ the
verb

snow until it looks just right. Now, it's time for

hot chocolate!

Emma Enters the Science Fair

"Hi Max," Emma said. She sat next to him on the bus. "Look what I got at school today." She gave him a paper.

"There is a science fair next week?" Max asked. "That sounds cool! Are you entering?"

"Of course!" Emma said. Emma loved science.

Directions: Look at the science fair flyer. Some words are missing. Circle the correctly spelled word.

SCIENCE FAIR

_____ May 18, 2012   Fryday Friday

Weston Elementary School

5 P.M.

First _____ is a new bike!   prize prise

Science is _____! fan fun

"What are you going to make?" Max asked.

"A volcano," Emma said. "We learned about them last week."

"That sounds fun!" Max said.

"Will you help me paint it?" Emma asked. Max was a great artist.

"Sure," Max said. "Let's get started."

Directions: Help Max and Emma find the supplies they need. Look at the words in the box. Find and circle them in the picture.

paint	empty bottle	bowl
glue	newspaper	

Max and Emma worked hard on the volcano. Emma built it. Max painted it.

"This looks good," Emma said. "It needs to dry for a day. Then, I can add the big surprise!"

"What surprise?" Max wanted to know.

"My mom is going to help me make it erupt," Emma said. "I get to make a mixture in my lab!"

Directions: Help Max and Emma finish the volcano. Color it.

The day of the science fair quickly arrived. Emma was nervous, but excited. Max came, too.

Emma added the special mixture to her volcano. It erupted!

"I'm glad that worked," Emma said. "I will find out if I won tomorrow."

"Good luck, Emma!" Max said.

Directions: Finish the story. Did Emma win? Draw your ending.

Directions: Review the story. Write your answers on the lines.

What is Emma's favorite school subject?

art   science

What day of the week is the science fair on?

_____

What is your favorite school subject?

_____

Name two things you need to make a volcano.

_____

_____

Language Arts in Science

spring

summer

autumn

winter

Liquids and Solids

Matter is everywhere. Everything on Earth is made of matter. There are three types of matter: liquids, solids, and gases.

A **liquid** does not have a shape. Water is a liquid. Can you think of another liquid? Draw it.

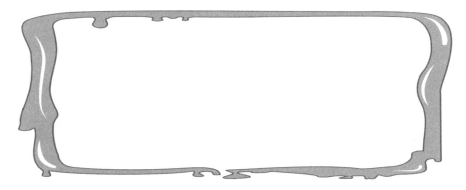

A **solid** has a shape. Many things are solids, such as tables, apples, and you! Draw a solid.

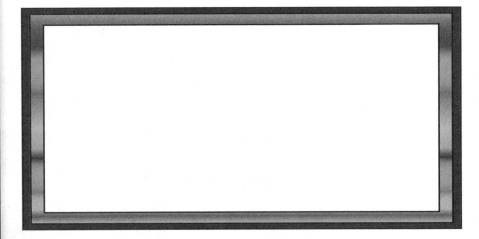

Weather Word Search

Directions: Look at the weather words in the box. Find them in the word search. Use **blue** to circle nouns and **red** to circle adjectives. Words can be up, down, across, or diagonal.

```
h  t  y  n  f  q  e  h  e  k  w  r
u  m  l  g  w  c  l  o  u  d  o  a
r  e  t  i  e  v  d  t  i  v  o  i
r  l  o  x  g  u  s  t  t  c  h  n
i  w  r  r  e  h  o  h  s  o  e  s
c  a  n  a  v  q  t  u  j  l  l  p
a  f  a  z  e  b  f  n  p  d  u  n
n  s  d  r  n  s  c  d  i  o  i  j
e  n  o  l  w  n  o  e  z  n  e  t
n  i  t  p  b  o  s  r  e  i  g  g
b  s  u  n  v  w  u  n  r  t  j  b
```

sun	cloud	thunder	snow	tornado
hurricane	hot	rain	cold	lightning

Weather: Clouds

There are three types of clouds: Cirrus, Cumulus, and Stratus. Each cloud is different. Read about the clouds below and follow the directions.

Cirrus clouds are high in the sky. They are white and feathery and contain ice crystals.

Directions: What words describe Cirrus clouds?

_____

_____

Cumulus clouds are low in the sky. They are puffy and white, like cotton balls.

Directions: What words describe Cumulus clouds?

_____

_____

Stratus clouds are low in the sky. They are wide, often gray, and bring snow and rain.

Directions: What words describe Stratus clouds?

_____

_____

Four Seasons

Directions: Draw a line to match each picture to the correct season. Fill in the missing letter in each season. Use the words in the box to help you.

spring   summer   winter   autumn

s_ring

win_er

sum_er

au_umn

The Sun

Directions: Read about the Sun. Then, complete the crossword puzzle on page 65.

The Sun is a star. It is the center of our solar system. The planets travel around the Sun. The Sun is made up of gases. Hydrogen makes up most of the Sun, but it also contains a lot of helium.

The Sun makes its own light. The Sun shines and makes plants grow. The Sun also gives off heat. It keeps us warm. It is the nearest star to Earth. We could not live without the Sun.

Directions: Unscramble the words below. Then, fill in the blanks.

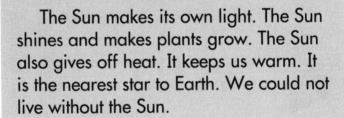

astr   asgse   mraw

The Sun is a_____.

The Sun is made of_____.

The Sun keeps us_____.

64

Sunny Crossword

Directions: Complete the puzzle. Use page 64 to help. One is done for you.

Across

3. The Sun is the center of the ____ system.

4. The Sun is mostly made of ____.

6. The Sun also contains ____.

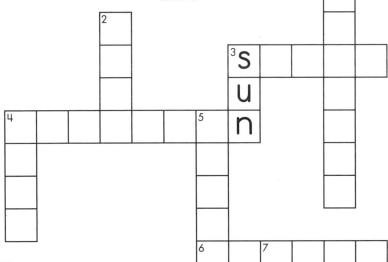

Down

1. The ____ travel around the Sun.

2. The Sun is a ____.

3. We could not live without the ____.

4. The Sun gives off ____.

5. The Sun is the nearest star to ____.

7. The Sun makes its own ____.

The Moon

Max is pretending he is going to the moon! First, he reads about three important surfaces of the moon.

Directions: Read about the moon with Max.

Earth has one moon. You can see the moon in the sky. The moon travels around Earth. It is closer to Earth than the Sun or planets. But the moon is much smaller than Earth.

The surface of the moon has many deep holes called **craters**. It has flat areas called **maria** and rocky mountain areas called **highlands**. The moon has no air, water, or life.

Directions: Write two sentences to describe the moon. Use capital letters and periods.

_____

_____

_____

_____

_____

_____

Earth

Directions: Read about Earth. Some words are missing. Use the words from the box to complete the paragraph.

Sun	closer	soil	Earth

The third planet from the _____ is our planet Earth. Earth is at the right distance from the Sun to have the liquid water necessary to support life. Mercury and Venus are too hot because they are _____ to the Sun. The other planets are too far from the Sun.

Earth has a lot of water. Most living things need water. Water helps to control Earth's weather and climate. Water also breaks rock into _____, which plants need to grow.

_____ is a special planet!

Edible Earth

Make a model of Earth's layers that is good enough to eat! Read about the three layers below. Then, answer the questions on page 69.

What you'll need:
- A bag of marshmallows
- Hazelnuts or hard candy
- Melted chocolate
- An adult

The **core** is the inner layer of Earth. The core is solid and very hot.

Surrounding the core is the **mantle**. The mantle is the largest layer. It separates the core from the crust.

The **crust** is the outer shell of Earth. It is the thinnest layer, but it is very hard. We live on the crust!

Edible Earth

What to do:

1. Select one marshmallow. The marshmallow will represent the **mantle**.

2. Put a hazelnut or piece of hard candy into the center of the marshmallow.

   What layer does the hazelnut represent?

   _____

3. Then, dip the marshmallow into melted chocolate.

   What layer does the chocolate represent?

   _____

4. Enjoy your snack and teach your friends and family about Earth's three layers.

What layer do we live on? _____

What is the hottest layer? _____

Parts of a Plant

Directions: Read the passage. Label the parts of a plant. Use the words in the box to help you.

All plants begin from **seeds**. The **roots** are in the ground and suck up water. The plant's **stem** is above the ground. **Leaves** grow off of the stem. Sometimes, a plant has a **flower** on top of the stem. **Buds** are small flowers that have not finished growing yet.

bud	flower	stem
leaf	seed	root

Paper Mâché Volcano

Emma wants to teach you how to make your own volcano! This fun science project will take a few days to prepare. But, when you are finished, you will have your own steaming volcano. Ask an adult to help you.

What you'll need:
- Large piece of cardboard
- Plastic bottle
- Newspaper
- Glue
- Sticky tape
- Paint
- Sand, pebbles, moss (optional)
- An adult

Paper Mâché Volcano

What to do:

1. Tape the empty plastic bottle to the middle of the cardboard, as shown. Then, begin gluing newspaper to the bottle.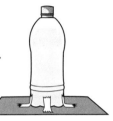

2. Use crumpled newspaper to form a cone around the plastic bottle.

3. Mix glue with a little water until it is sticky, but liquid.

4. Next, cut or tear more newspaper into small square pieces. Dip the pieces of newspaper in the glue mixture and place them on the cone.

5. You will want several layers of newspaper around the cone, so let each layer fully dry before adding another.

6. Continue to form a dome shape around the plastic bottle until your volcano is the size you want.

Once your volcano is dry, it is time to paint it. Max has a few tips about painting your volcano.

1. Choose paints that are waterproof when dry—such as acrylic paint.

2. When you paint, use the brush to create texture, instead of smooth paint lines. This will make your volcano look rough and rocky—just like real volcanoes.

3. You can even glue some real sand, pebbles, or moss to your cardboard to make it look like a forest.

Paper Mâché Volcano

Ask an adult to help you carefully follow the instructions below to create an exciting eruption.

1. Pour baking soda into the bottle inside the volcano. The bottle represents the lava chamber (fill up about a fourth of the bottle).

2. Pour vinegar into a regular drinking glass.

3. Mix red food coloring with the vinegar (optional: you can also add a little starch to the vinegar).

4. Slowly, pour the vinegar mixture into the bottle. The vinegar will react with the baking soda to create an eruption!

Observe your volcano's eruption! Describe it using adjectives below.

_____

_____

_____

_____

_____

Language Arts in Crafts

NEWS TEAM

Monster Sock Puppet

Turn your sock into a monster! Make your monster any animal or creature imaginable. Be creative! Give your monster a name and write a story about it on page 77.

What you'll need:
- Sock
- **Red** felt or fabric oval
- Fabric scraps (any colors)
- Fabric scissors
- Craft glue (try to use glue made especially for fabric)

What to do:

1. Put one hand in the sock to find where the mouth should be. Your thumb should make the bottom jaw of the monster's mouth. Glue the **red** fabric oval where the mouth is formed.

2. Cut out eyes, ears, and anything else you want on your monster from fabric scraps and glue them on your monster.

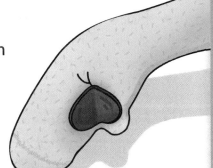

3. Fill in the blanks below with silly adjectives to tell a story about your monster.

One day, a _____ monster jumped out

in front of me! It had _____ eyes and a

_____ roar. I took it to school. That was the

_____ show and tell my class had ever seen!

Create a Stage

Put on a puppet show and learn about story structure by following some of these great tips!

- Place a low table in front of a chalkboard or a large sheet of butcher paper taped to the wall. Draw a scene on the board or paper, like a farm. This is your **setting**.

- Drape a sheet or blanket around the table. Sit beneath the table with your puppets to begin the show.

- Use any types of puppets as your **characters**.

- Make sure your story has a **sequence**. There should be a beginning, middle, and end.

- Have a friend help you put on a show for your family! Be sure to give your play a title.

A TV Show

Read about Emma's science fair beginning on page 53. Who did you decide won the science fair on page 57? Follow the steps below to make a TV. Then, fill in the blanks to make a news broadcast about the winner of the science fair!

- Cut out a rectangular hole in the bottom of a large cardboard box. Draw features such as buttons and decorate the rest of the box.

- Set the TV on a table that has been draped with a sheet or blanket. Get behind the box to perform on TV.

Good evening. Tonight's top story is about the winner

of the Weston Elementary science fair. _____

won the science fair with an amazing project about

_____. It took the winner _____ hours

to make the project!

Puffy Paint

Use puffy paint to make three-dimensional pictures!
You can also use it to create alphabet flashcards for
a fun language arts game.

What you'll need:

- $\frac{1}{2}$ cup flour
- $\frac{1}{2}$ cup salt
- About 1 cup water
- Plastic squeeze
  bottle (a clean honey
  dispenser works
  well)
- 4 or 5 teaspoons
  tempera paint
- Paintbrushes
- Paper
- Mixing bowl
- Funnel (optional)

What to do:

1. Stir together the flour, salt, and about half the water in a bowl.

2. Add the tempera paint.

3. Slowly, add more water until the mixture can be poured, but is not runny.

4. Use the funnel to pour the mixture into a squeeze bottle.

5. Squeeze the paint onto paper. Let the picture dry for several hours.

Suggestion

- Play a game with touch and feel alphabet cards. Write one large letter using puffy paint on an index card. Then, place all the cards in a paper bag. Take turns reaching into the bag and trying to identify the letter by touch. For an extra challenge, you have 10 seconds to name something that starts with that letter!

Treasure Map

Get ready for adventure! Make your own treasure map using simple household items. It is just like Max's map!

What you'll need:
- White paper
- $\frac{1}{2}$ cup of cold coffee or tea
- Blow-dryer
- Cookie sheet or large plate
- Markers or crayons

What to do:

1. Rip the edges off of the white paper and crumble it into a ball. Then, flatten it back out.

2. Lay the paper on a cookie sheet or plate. Pour or dab the coffee or tea all over the paper. Let it sit and absorb the stains for five minutes before you pour off the extra liquid.

3. Blow dry the paper on the cookie sheet for about five minutes or until it is dry enough to color on.

4. Draw your map with markers and crayons.

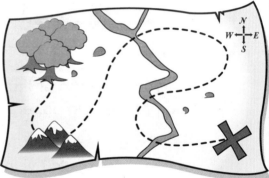

Read "Max's Map" starting on page 5. Make a map for a friend and write some simple steps for them to follow, like the ones on page 7. Write your steps below.

_____

_____

_____

_____

_____

_____

Thumbprint Animal Comic

Use your thumbprints to make any animal!
Practice making your favorite animals
on a separate sheet of paper. Then,
when you are ready, use them to
illustrate your own original comic below!

What you'll need:
- Several stamp pads
- Paper
- Crayons, markers,
  or colored pencils

What to do:

1. Roll your fingertip or thumb over the stamp pad
   and press it onto paper.

2. Add the animal details (eyes, nose, ears,
   whiskers, teeth, etc.) with the crayons.
   Then, make your own comic!

Answer Key

frgiafe

giraffe

85

Page 6

"Hi Emma," Max called. "Look what I found in my backyard!"

"That looks like a pirate's map!" Emma said.

"Let's follow it and see where it goes," Max said.

"Maybe we will find treasure!" Emma said.

Directions: Color Max and Emma.

Colors will vary.

Page 7

"There are a lot of steps to follow," Max said.

"Let's start at the tree," Emma said. She pointed to the big tree in Max's backyard.

"Good idea," Max said. He carefully held the map. "First, we need to take 10 steps toward the swings."

Directions: Help Max and Emma read the map. Draw the path they should take. Follow the directions below.

Start at the tree. Walk to the swing set.

Next, walk past the doghouse.

Then, turn and walk around the **red** table.

Walk straight down to the gate.

Page 8

"Looks like we need to go through the gate," Max said.

"The treasure must be in my backyard!" Emma exclaimed. They walked into Emma's yard.

"Uh oh," Max said. "We have to cross a river!" He pointed toward the little pool for Emma's baby brother.

"Just like real pirates!" Emma said.

Directions: Imagine Max and Emma are pirates. Draw them crossing a river.

Drawings will vary.

Page 9

"Look!" called Emma. "X marks the spot!" She pointed to a big X drawn in the sandbox.

"Let's start digging," Max said excitedly.

"I found a treasure box," Max said. "And it has my name on it!"

"I wonder what is inside?" Emma asked with a smile.

Directions: What do you think Max's treasure is? Draw it in the treasure box.

Drawings will vary.

Page 10

"Did you like your pirate's map, Max?" asked Emma.

"Yeah! That was fun," Max said.

"Good, maybe I will make you another one," Emma said.

"You made the map?" Max laughed. "I want to make one for you first!"

Directions: Review the story. Write your answers on the lines.

Whose backyard does the map start in? (Max's) Emma's

What do Max and Emma pretend to be when they cross the pool? pirates

Who made the treasure map? Emma

Page 12

Crack the Code

Directions: Use Max and Emma's secret code to unlock a silly but true statement. A **statement** is a telling sentence that ends with a period (.). Add a period to the end of the statement after you break the code.

A	B	C	D	E	F	G	H	I	J	K	L	M

N	O	P	Q	R	S	T	U	V	W	X	Y	Z

A SNAIL

CAN SLEEP

FOR THREE

YEARS .

Space Nouns

Directions: Find the out-of-this-world space nouns from the word box. Remember, **nouns** name a person, place, or thing. Words can be across, down, or diagonal.

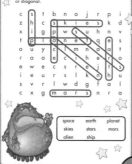

```
c s t b n o j r p i
z h c s k i e s k d
x i g p w s u h n v
t o p l a n e t q e
o u y c l m n a r h
r a a e c l h e o l
e w e c s r e j n h
i e u r s l k h s l
s v r l w d g f a l
c x g m a r s n r a
```

space	earth	planet
skies	stars	mars
alien	ship	

13

Hidden Picture

Directions: There are six nouns hidden in Max's backyard. Find and circle them. What other nouns do you see?

butterfly	apple	beach ball
baseball bat	frog	turtle

14

Crack the Code

Directions: Use Max and Emma's secret code to unlock the answer to a question. A **question** is an asking sentence that ends with a question mark (**?**). Fill in the missing question mark below. Then, solve the code to find the answer!

How do you take a sick pig to the hospital ?

A	B	C	D	E	F	G	H	I	J	K	L	M
N	O	P	Q	R	S	T	U	V	W	X	Y	Z

I N   A

H A M B U L A N C E

15

Spelling: Word Scramble

Directions: Look at the pictures and words. The words are all scrambled up! Spell the words correctly on the lines.

 rutkc   truck

 ynra   yarn

 frgiafe   giraffe

 likm   milk

16

Vowel Maze

Directions: Help Max answer a riddle. Follow the vowels **a**, **e**, **i**, **o**, and **u** through the maze to find the answer.

What kind of key will not open a door?

17

Crack the Code

Directions: Use Max and Emma's secret code to unlock the answer to a question. Fill in the missing punctuation for the question and answer.

Why did the banana go to the doctor ?

A	B	C	D	E	F	G	H	I	J	K	L	M
N	O	P	Q	R	S	T	U	V	W	X	Y	Z

I T   W A S   N O T

P E E L I N G

W E L L .

18

Proper Nouns

Directions: A **proper noun** names a special person, place, or thing. It starts with a capital letter. Read each riddle below. Find and unscramble the correct proper noun from the word box. Be sure to start with the capital letter!

rMas	rEath
nuS	nruSat

This huge star lights the day.

S u n

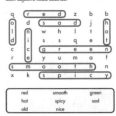

This is our home planet. E a r t h

This planet is red. M a r s

This planet has rings. S a t u r n

19

Adjective Word Search

An **adjective** is a word that describes a noun. It tells more about a noun, like **yellow** duck or **hard** rock. Adjectives can answer the question **what kind?**

Directions: Find the adjectives from the word box. Words can be across or down. Then, think of a noun each adjective could describe.

```
q   r   e   d   z   b   b
o   d   s   a   d   j   h
l   n   w   h   l   t   o
d   i   s   s   q   e   t
c   c   g   r   e   e   n
r   e   y   u   m   a   f
s   m   o   o   t   h   n
x   k   s   p   i   c   y
```

red	smooth	green
hot	spicy	sad
old	nice	

20

On the Playground

When writing sentences, it is important to use **subject-verb agreement**. When a sentence is about one person or thing, add **s** to the verb, such as the leaf blow**s** away. When a sentence is about more than one person or thing, do not add **s** to the verb, such as the cats look for mice.

Directions: Fill in the verbs below with your own silly ideas. Then, write them in the story. Be sure to use correct subject-verb agreement.

Verb (action word) _____

Verb (action word) _____   *Answers will vary.*

Verb (action word) _____

Finally, the recess bell rings! First, Emma

_____ to the swings. Max
  verb
and his friends start a game of tag. Max

_____ right into Emma! Then,
  verb
Max and Emma _____ a ball
  verb
back and forth before it's time to go back inside.

21

Spelling: Word Scramble

Directions: Look at the pictures and words. The words are all scrambled up! Spell the words correctly on the lines.

 gsrsa — grass

 rebda — bread

 pzirep — zipper

 hrtea — heart

22

Crossword Puzzle

Directions: A **noun** is a person, place, or thing. A **verb** is an action word, like **jump** or **swim**. Finish writing the nouns and verbs from the word box in the puzzle. Circle the nouns in blue and the verbs in green.

ran	last	legs	digs
gate	camp	rest	sip
sat	pen	end	kick

23

Riddles

Directions: An **adjective** describes a noun. It tells more about a noun, like **big** dog. Read the riddles below. Circle the adjectives. Then, draw a line from the riddle to the answer.

My big body is heavy.
I lived a long, long time ago.
What am I?

My tall neck is long.
I eat leaves from trees.
What am I?

I have long ears.
I hop very fast.
What am I?

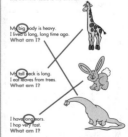

24

Space Nouns

Directions: Find the out-of-this-world space nouns from the word box. Words can be across or down.

```
o  i  t  w  s  m  c  v  j  k
g  a  l  a  x  y  l  o  l  p
s  b  c  g  p  c  t  m  a  n
n  k  s  p  g  e  r  c  s  s
w  v  l  b  r  o  c  k  e  t
u  f  o  u  i  q  w  r  r  a
e  k  z  t  m  e  t  e  o  r
t  a  x  x  a  n  c  u  j  g
q  j  f  g  f  p  b  n  l  r
l  i  g  h  t  e  t  t  w  s
```

galaxy	rocket
laser	light
star	meteor

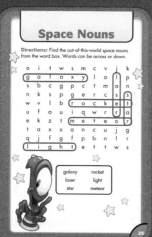

25

Max and Emma Go to the Fair

Directions: Fill in the nouns, adjectives, and verbs below with your own silly ideas. Then, write them in the story. Be sure to use correct subject-verb agreement.

Noun (a thing) _____

Verb (action word) _____

Adjective (describing word) _____

Answers will vary.

Max and Emma are at the fair. First, they go

see the _____. Max is so
            noun

excited he _____ the whole way
            verb

there! Emma stops to buy a _____
                        adjective

cotton candy. They love coming to the fair!

26

Matching Game

hat	bat
snake	rake
fan	pan
box	fox
spoon	moon

27

Matching Game

mop	top
flag	bag
clock	rock
log	dog

29

Crossword Puzzle

Directions: Finish writing the words from the word box in the puzzle below. Circle nouns in orange and verbs in purple.

bike	lake	feet	seed
ride	mule	bone	
gate	dive	rule	

```
      m u l e
      a
    b i k e
  b o n e
    n       f e
  r   e   d i v e   g a
  u               a t
  s e e d     r i d e
```

31

Animal Riddles

Directions: Draw a line from the riddle to the correct answer. Circle the verb in each sentence.

I love to slide on the ice.
What am I?

I slither on the ground because I have no arms or legs.
What am I?

I hop on lily pads in a pond with my webbed feet.
What am I?

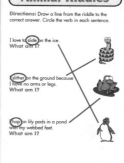

32

Crack the Code

Directions: Use Max and Emma's secret code to unlock the answer to a joke. An **exclamation** is a sentence that shows excitement or surprise. The answers to many jokes end with exclamation points (!). Add an exclamation point to the end of the sentence after you break the code.

Why was the baby ant confused?

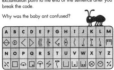

A	B	C	D	E	F	G	H	I	J	K	L	M

N	O	P	Q	R	S	T	U	V	W	X	Y	Z

A L L   H I S

U N C L E S

W E R E   A N T S !

33

Maze

Directions: Help Emma answer a riddle. Draw a line through the maze to find the answer. What other adjectives could describe the answer?

What is orange and sounds like **parrot**?

34

Reveal Hidden Picture

Directions: Color all of the vowels **a, e, i, o,** and **u black** to discover something hidden in the puzzle.

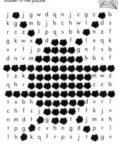

35

Crossword

Directions: Finish writing the words from the word box in the puzzle below. Use **blue** to circle nouns, to circle verbs, and **red** to circle adjectives.

cat	pops	song	zoo
fog	fan	pear	tan
car	pig	hop	blue

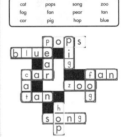

36

Matching Contractions

A contraction is a way to join two words together. It is a shorter way to say something. An apostrophe (') takes the place of the missing letters. For example, **isn't** is a contraction of the words **is not**.

Directions: Draw a line to match each pair of words to its contraction.

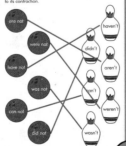

- are not
- were not
- have not
- was not
- can not
- did not

- haven't
- didn't
- aren't
- can't
- weren't
- wasn't

37

Spelling: Word Scramble

Directions: Look at the pictures and words. The words are all scrambled up! Spell the words correctly on the lines.

pgersa — grapes

mneoyk — monkey

olgio — igloo

grof — frog

38

90

Max's Invention

Directions: Fill in the nouns, adjectives, and verbs below with your own silly ideas. Then, write them in the story. Be sure to use correct subject-verb agreement!

Noun (a thing) _____

Adjective (describing word) _____ *Answers*

Verb (action word) _____ *will vary.*

Adjective (describing word) _____

Max made an invention to help feed his dog.

He used _____, duct tape,
           noun
and rope to make it. Emma came over to see his

_____ invention. Max and
   adjective

Emma _____ it outside.
       verb

His _____ dog sniffs it.
     adjective

Now, Max just needs to test it out!

39

Crossword Puzzle: Synonyms

Directions: **Synonyms** are words that mean the same or almost the same thing, like **dad** and **father**. Write the synonyms in the puzzle below. Use the word box to help you.

Puzzle answers:
- fast (down)
- hop (down)
- happy
- shout
- sleepy

Across
5. synonym of **yell**
6. synonym of **tired**

Down
1. synonym of **quick**
2. synonym of **small**
3. synonym of **leap**
4. synonym of **glad**

fast	hop	little
shout	sleepy	happy

40

Maze

Emma has a riddle for you! See if you can find the answer.

Directions: Solve Emma's riddle. Draw a line through the maze to find the answer.

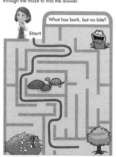

What has bark, but no bite?

Start

41

Verb Word Search

A **verb** is an action word. It tells what happens in a sentence, like Max **kicks** the ball or Emma **laughs** at the joke.

Directions: Find the verbs from the word box. Words can be across or down. Then, try to use each verb in a sentence.

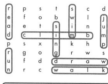

walk	swim	climb
sing	draw	run
read	jump	

42

Riddles

Directions: Read the riddles below. Circle the adjectives. Then, draw a line from the riddle to the answer.

I have eight long arms.
I can blend in with the ocean floor.
What am I?

I am a very slow swimmer.
My short tail pushes me through the water upright.
What am I?

I have very sharp teeth.
If you see my fin in the water, swim away.
What am I?

43

Crossword Puzzle

Directions: **Synonyms** are words that mean the same thing, like **glad** and **happy**. **Antonyms** are words that are opposites, like **yes** and **no**. Write the antonyms in the puzzle below. Use the word box to help you.

Puzzle answers: high, heavy, yes, safe, full, left, tight

Across
1. antonym of **low**
2. antonym of **no**
4. antonym of **empty**
6. antonym of **loose**

Down
1. antonym of **light**
3. antonym of **dangerous**
5. antonym of **right**

high	safe	left	full
heavy	yes	tight	

44

Hidden Picture

Directions: There are eight nouns hidden in the jellybeans. Find and circle them.

orange	pencil	strawberry
cherry	sharpener	tennis ball
cookie	pink bow	blue marble

45

Tongue Twisters

Directions: Read the tongue twisters below out loud. Can you say them fast three times? Then, write your own tongue twister on the lines!

She sells seashells by the sea shore

Black background, **brown** background

Black back bat

Six slimy snails sailed silently

Answers will vary.

_____

46

Word Search

Directions: Use a **red** crayon to circle the names of three animals that would make good pets. Use a **blue** crayon to circle the names of three wild animals. Use an **orange** crayon to circle two animals that live on a farm. Words can be across or down.

bear	lion	bird	cow
cat	sheep	dog	tiger

```
a m e o w w n (l i o n)
b m (d o g) g x i i s o
a (b e a r) r v l m h r
r m r m o o u s e e k
k  c a b (b i r d) s e m
i  o t (t i g e r) m p q
b  w n o w w r q n e n
d  n c p h h i d u d n
f  k (c a t) t r o a r m
```

47

Emma's New Pet

Directions: Fill in the nouns, adjectives, and verbs below with your own silly ideas. Then, write them in the story. Be sure to use correct subject-verb agreement!

Noun (animal) _____

Adjective (describing word) _____

Verb (action word) _____

Noun (thing) _____

Answers will vary.

Emma has a new pet. It is a _____!
                                    noun

Max is playing with it, too. He gives the pet a

_____ toy. Emma _____
   adjective   verb

with her new pet. She gives it a new

_____. Now, it just needs a name.
   noun

48

Vowel Maze

Directions: Follow the vowels **a, e, i, o,** and **u** through the maze to help the monkey find the bananas.

49

Spelling: Word Scramble

Directions: Look at the pictures and words. The words are all scrambled up! Spell the words correctly on the lines.

enska	snake
clcok	clock
apepl	apple
eter	tree

50

92

Card 51

Create Your Own Sentence

Max and Emma want you to write a secret sentence! Give your coded sentence to a friend.

Directions: Use Max and Emma's code key to create your own secret sentence in the space below. Be sure to end it with a period, question mark, or exclamation point.

A	B	C	D	E	F	G	H	I	J	K	L	M
N	O	P	Q	R	S	T	U	V	W	X	Y	Z

Answers will vary.

51

Card 52

Snow Day!

Directions: Fill in the nouns, adjectives, and verbs below with your own silly ideas. Then, write them in the story. Be sure to use correct subject-verb agreement!

Adjective (describing word) _____

Verb (action word) _____

Answers

Noun (person or thing) _____

will vary.

Verb (action word) _____

Max looks out the window, it snowed last night and school is cancelled! He runs outside to play

in the _____ snow. Emma
      adjective

_____ outside. They start
      verb

building a _____ out of
      noun

snow. They _____ the
      verb

snow until it looks just right. Now, it's time for

hot chocolate!

52

Card 54

"Hi Max," Emma said. She sat next to him on the bus. "Look what I got at school today." She gave him a paper.

"There is a science fair next week?" Max asked. "That sounds cool! Are you entering?"

"Of course!" Emma said. Emma loved science.

Directions: Look at the science fair flyer. Some words are missing. Circle the correctly spelled word.

SCIENCE FAIR

_____ May 18, 2012 Fryday Friday

Weston Elementary School

5 P.M.

First _____ is a new bike! prize prise

Science is _____! fun funn

54

Card 55

"What are you going to make?" Max asked.

"A volcano," Emma said. "We learned about them last week."

"That sounds fun!" Max said.

"Will you help me paint it?" Emma asked. Max was a great artist.

"Sure," Max said. "Let's get started."

Directions: Help Max and Emma find the supplies they need. Look at the words in the box. Find and circle them in the picture.

paint	empty bottle	bowl
glue	newspaper	

55

Card 56

Max and Emma worked hard on the volcano. Emma built it. Max painted it.

"This looks good," Emma said. "It needs to dry for a day. Then, I can add the big surprise!"

"What surprise?" Max wanted to know.

"My mom is going to help me make it erupt," Emma said. "I get to make a mixture in my lab!"

Directions: Help Max and Emma finish the volcano. Color it.

Drawings will vary.

56

Card 57

The day of the science fair quickly arrived. Emma was nervous, but excited. Max came, too.

Emma added the special mixture to her volcano. It erupted!

"I'm glad that worked," Emma said. "I will find out if I won tomorrow."

"Good luck, Emma!" Max said.

Directions: Finish the story. Did Emma win? Draw your ending.

Drawings will vary.

57

Card 58

Directions: Review the story. Write your answers on the lines.

What is Emma's favorite school subject?

art (science)

What day of the week is the science fair on?

Friday

What is your favorite school subject?

Answers will vary.

Name two things you need to make a volcano.

Answers may include:
Paint, glue, empty bottle,
newspaper, or bowl

58

Card 60

Liquids and Solids

Matter is everywhere. Everything on Earth is made of matter. There are three types of matter: liquids, solids, and gases.

A **liquid** does not have a shape. Water is a liquid. Can you think of another liquid? Draw it.

> Drawings will vary.

A **solid** has a shape. Many things are solids, such as tables, apples, and you! Draw a solid.

> Drawings will vary.

60

Card 61

Weather Word Search

Directions: Look at the weather words in the box. Find them in the word search. Use blue to circle nouns and red to circle adjectives. Words can be up, down, across, or diagonal.

```
h  t  y  n  f  q  e  h  e  k  w  r
u  m  g  w  c  l  o  u  d  o  a  o
r  e  t  i  e  v  d  t  i  v  o  i
r  l  o  x  g  u  s  t  t  c  h  n
i  w  r  r  e  h  o  h  s  o  e  s
c  a  n  a  v  q  f  u  j  l  d  j
a  f  a  z  e  b  f  n  p  d  u  n
n  s  d  r  n  s  c  d  r  o  i  j
e  n  o  l  w  n  o  e  z  n  e  t
n  i  t  p  b  o  s  r  e  i  g  g
b  s  u  n  v  w  u  n  r  t  j  b
```

| sun | cloud | thunder | snow | tornado |
| hurricane | hot | rain | cold | lightning |

61

Card 62

Weather: Clouds

There are three types of clouds: Cirrus, Cumulus, and Stratus. Each cloud is different. Read about the clouds below and follow the directions.

Cirrus clouds are high in the sky. They are white and feathery and contain ice crystals.

Directions: What words describe Cirrus clouds?

Answers will vary.

Cumulus clouds are low in the sky. They are puffy and white, like cotton balls.

Directions: What words describe Cumulus clouds?

Answers will vary.

Stratus clouds are low in the sky. They are wide, often gray, and bring snow and rain.

Directions: What words describe Stratus clouds?

Answers will vary.

62

Card 63

Four Seasons

Directions: Draw a line to match each picture to the correct season. Fill in the missing letter in each season. Use the words in the box to help you.

| spring | summer | winter | autumn |

s_p_ring

win_t_er

summ_e_r

au_t_umn

63

Card 64

The Sun

Directions: Read about the Sun. Then, complete the crossword puzzle on page 65.

The Sun is a star. It is the center of our solar system. The planets travel around the Sun. The Sun is made up of gases. Hydrogen makes up most of it, but it also contains a lot of helium.

The Sun makes its own light. The Sun shines and makes plants grow. The Sun also gives off heat. It keeps us warm. It is the nearest star to Earth. We could not live without the Sun.

Directions: Unscramble the words below. Then, fill in the blanks.

| astr | asgse | mraw |

The Sun is a _star_

The Sun is made of _gases_

The Sun keeps us _warm_

64

Sunny Crossword

Directions: Complete the puzzle. Use page 64 to help. One is done for you.

Across

3. The Sun is the center of the ____ system.
4. The Sun is mostly made of ____.
6. The Sun also contains ____.

Crossword answers:
- planets
- star
- solar
- sun
- hydrogen
- heat
- part
- stars
- helium
- light

Down

1. The ____ travel around the Sun.
2. The Sun is a ____.
3. We could not live without the ____.
4. The Sun gives off ____.
5. The Sun is the nearest star to ____.
7. The Sun makes its own ____.

65

The Moon

Max is pretending he is going to the moon! First, he reads about three important surfaces of the moon.

Directions: Read about the moon with Max.

Earth has one moon. You can see the moon in the sky. The moon travels around Earth. It is closer to Earth than the Sun or planets. But the moon is much smaller than Earth.

The surface of the moon has many deep holes called **craters**. It has flat areas called **maria** and rocky mountain areas called **highlands**. The moon has no air, water, or life.

Directions: Write two sentences to describe the moon. Use capital letters and periods.

Answers will vary.

66

Earth

Directions: Read about Earth. Some words are missing. Use the words from the box to complete the paragraph.

| Sun | closer | soil | Earth |

The third planet from the __Sun__ is our planet Earth. Earth is at the right distance from the Sun to have the liquid water necessary to support life. Mercury and Venus are too hot because they are __closer__ to the Sun. The other planets are too far from the Sun.

Earth has a lot of water. Most living things need water. Water helps to control Earth's weather and climate. Water also breaks rock into __soil__, which plants need to grow.

__Earth__ is a special planet!

67

Edible Earth

What to do:

1. Select one marshmallow. The marshmallow will represent the **mantle**.

2. Put a hazelnut or piece of hard candy into the center of the marshmallow.

   What layer does the hazelnut represent? __core__

3. Then, dip the marshmallow into melted chocolate.

   What layer does the chocolate represent? __crust__

4. Enjoy your snack and teach your friends and family about Earth's three layers.

What layer do we live on? __crust__

What is the hottest layer? __core__

69

Parts of a Plant

Directions: Read the passage. Label the parts of a plant. Use the words in the box to help you.

All plants begin from **seeds**. The **roots** are in the ground and suck up water. The plant's **stem** is above the ground. **Leaves** grow off of the stem. Sometimes, a plant has a **flower** on top of the stem. **Buds** are small flowers that have not finished growing yet.

| bud | flower | stem |
| leaf | seed | root |

- flower
- seed
- bud
- leaf
- stem
- root

70

Paper Mâché Volcano

Ask an adult to help you carefully follow the instructions below to create an exciting eruption.

1. Pour baking soda into the bottle inside the volcano. The bottle represents the lava chamber (fill up about a fourth of the bottle).

2. Pour vinegar into a regular drinking glass.

3. Mix red food coloring with the vinegar (optional; you can also add a little starch to the vinegar).

4. Slowly, pour the vinegar mixture into the bottle. The vinegar will react with the baking soda to create an eruption!

Observe your volcano's eruption! Describe it using adjectives below.

Answers will vary.

74

What to do:

1. Put one hand in the sock to find where the mouth should be. Your thumb should make the bottom jaw of the monster's mouth. Glue the red fabric oval where the mouth is formed.

2. Cut out eyes, ears, and anything else you want on your monster from fabric scraps and glue them on your monster.

3. Fill in the blanks below with silly adjectives to tell a story about your monster.

One day, a _____ monster jumped out in front of me! It had _____ eyes and a _____ roar. I took it to school. That was the _____ show and tell my class had ever seen!

Answers will vary.

77

Read about Emma's science fair beginning on page 53. Who did you decide won the science fair on page 57? Follow the steps below to make a TV. Then, fill in the blanks to make a news broadcast about the winner of the science fair!

A TV Show

- Cut out a rectangular hole in the bottom of a large cardboard box. Draw features such as buttons and decorate the rest of the box.

- Set the TV on a table that has been draped with a sheet or blanket. Get behind the box to perform on TV.

Good evening. Tonight's top story is about the winner of the Weston Elementary science fair. _____ won the science fair with an amazing project about _____. It took the winner _____ hours to make the project!

Answers will vary.

NEWS TEAM

79

What to do:

1. Rip the edges off of the white paper and crumble it into a ball. Then, flatten it back out.

2. Lay the paper on a cookie sheet or plate. Pour or dab the coffee or tea all over the paper. Let it sit and absorb the stains for five minutes before you pour off the extra liquid.

3. Blow dry the paper on the cookie sheet for about five minutes or until it is dry enough to color on.

4. Draw your map with markers and crayons.

Read "Max's Map" starting on page 5. Make a map for a friend and write some simple steps for them to follow, like the ones on page 7. Write your steps below.

Answers will vary.

83

Thumbprint Animal Comic

Use your thumbprints to make any animal! Practice making your favorite animals on a separate sheet of paper. Then, when you are ready, use them to illustrate your own original comic below!

What you'll need:
- Several stamp pads
- Paper
- Crayons, markers, or colored pencils

What to do:

1. Roll your fingertip or thumb over the stamp pad and press it onto paper.

2. Add the animal details (eyes, nose, ears, whiskers, teeth, etc.) with the crayons. Then, make your own comic!

Drawings will vary.

84